How to Make a Sock Puppet

Written by Jillian Powell
Photographs by Steve Lumb

Collins

Pull the sock on.

Tuck the sock in.

Cut the tongue out.

Stick the tongue on.

Draw the eyes on.

Stick the eyes on.

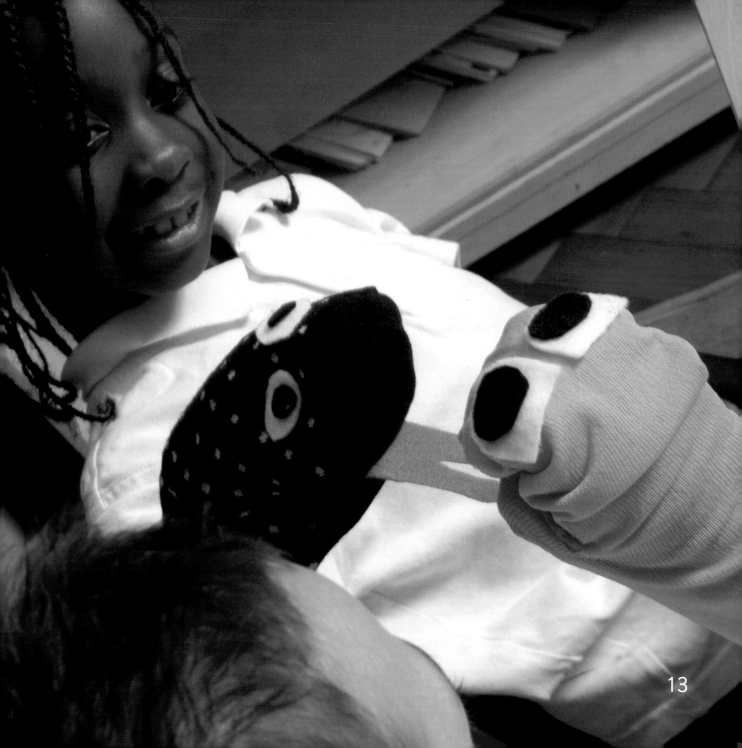

Making a sock puppet

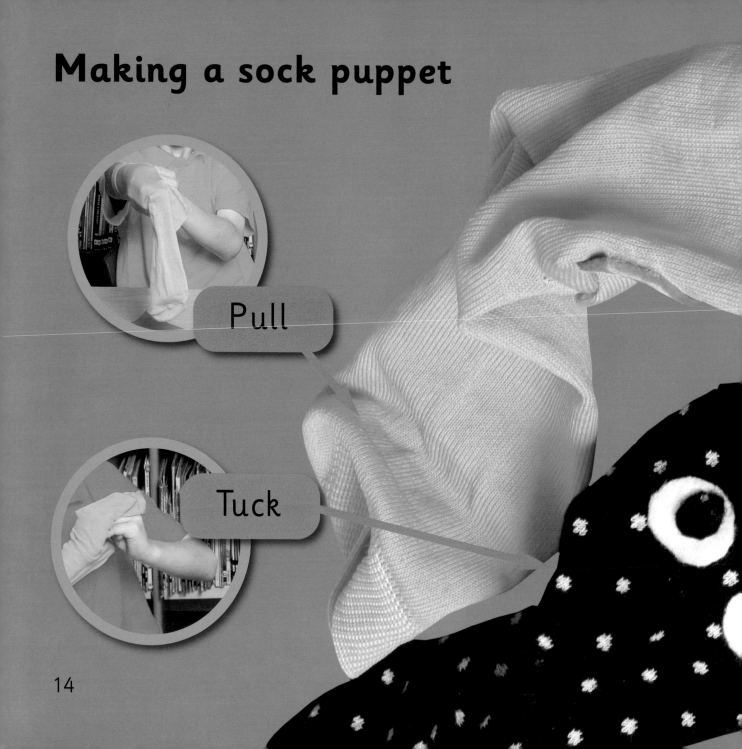

Pull

Tuck

Stick

Draw

Cut

15

Ideas for guided reading

Learning objectives: interact with others, negotiating plans and activities and taking turns in conversation; read a range of familiar and common words and simple sentences independently; show an understanding of how information can be found in non-fiction texts to answer questions about where, who, why and how

Curriculum links: Creative Development: Explore colour, texture, shape, form and space in two or three dimensions

High frequency words: on, the, in

Interest words: sock puppet, pull, stick, draw, cut, tuck, tongue, eyes

Word count: 29

Resources: ready-made sock puppet, socks, coloured paper, glue, scissors, felt-tip pens

Getting started

- Show the children a sock puppet. Ask them to explain what it is and how it works.
- Explain that they are going to read an instruction book that will teach them how to make their own sock puppets.
- Give out the books and ask the children to read the front and back covers.
- Ask the children to find all the action words (verbs) in the blurb, e.g. *make, cut, glue.* Invite children to suggest other action words that might appear in this instruction book.

Reading and responding

- In pairs, ask children to read the book all the way through, trying to follow the instructions.
- Remind children of the range of strategies that they can use to decode new words: sounding out, using the pictures for clues, using the sense of the sentence.